Thank you for your support!

Braille Code Inc.

www.brailecodeclothing.com
braillecodebrands@gmail.com

DEDICATION

I dedicate this book to my children: Wani, Niara and Zaire who no matter how old you get, you will always be my babies! Mami Loves You So Much!! Wani, you came into my world, you gave it purpose and life! We became a team, we learned how to live with your visual impairment and we excelled!! I am so proud of what we've done buddy! We are going to show the world that we won with God, through faith, prayers and love! Niara, you are mama's most prettiest girl! You are such a caring little girl with so much personality, you are my hearts joy! Baby Zaire, you're only a few months and you have filled my life with such happiness, you are so sweet and yummy! To my husband, my babe Dwayne Anthony Cane. You've been my ultimate support in all my endeavors! You are my dude, my best friend and the man that I will always Love! I can't thank you enough for all you've done for me and Braille Code. As we always say: "Teamwork Make Dreams Work" and we are doing IT! I love you. Last but not least, my brother, my confidant Pablo Benedith for always being there to lend an ear, you've been with me from the start cheering me on and helping me through every aspect of my business, love you Beedo.

THANK YOU

My best friends/siblings, Pablo, Betsy, Kim, Carly and Debbie for always encouraging me through my passion and telling me to Never give up! I also want to thank Wilson Moreira. Wilson, for your continued support, I will forever be grateful for your encouragement regarding Braille Code and reminding me to keep a tough skin in this business game. Dennis Morgan for creating the 3 blind mice with me. My sister-in-law Kia Cane and my parents-in-law Dennis Cane and Sheila Johnson for your love and awesome food :-). Marie, for your love and belief in Braille Code from the start. To my friends: Dupé Ajayi and Mariano (Juni) Martinez: thank you for your business advice and being there for every aspect of Braille Code's growth. Jocelyn Martinez, Ana Peña, Ms. Sacoyia and Allison Samuel Wong: you have been so gracious to me and my family, for that we are very thankful. My loving cousin/sister in Christ Lorraine Benedict and Edson Garcia, I can't thank you both enough for learning about Braille Code and jumping on board to make things happen! Love you all!

THANK YOU MAMI Graciela Benedith... The leading lady of my life! Eres unica! Por tu amor! Por siempre dándome la fuerza cuando lo necesitaba. Sobre todo, te doy las gracias por darme Dios. Te quiero eternamente Señora Grace!

To my attorneys: Sara Skinner-Chubb and Robert Newman.

THANK YOU GOD for Everything! For choosing me to create Braille Code and for starting it all off with Your gift, my son Wani! I Love You!

Yes, the Lord has done great things for us, and we are filled with joy!
Psalm 126:3

In Loving Memory of Pablo Hernan Benedith, Sr.

Photo by: Mr. G

I thank you eternally for being the absolute greatest father. You gave me integrity, humility and creativity. Most of all you taught me how to love because you were my first love. Papi, you are my inspiration, my strength and you gave me the courage to do all things.

I Love You and miss you so much.

INTRODUCTION AND IMPORTANT NOTICE ABOUT THE THREE BLIND MICE:

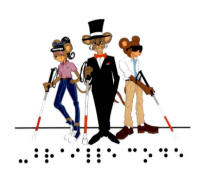

In 2014, my friend Morgan and I were on the phone trying to figure out what mascots would represent my company Braille Code Inc. Morgan said that all brands have one or more mascots… that's when he came up with the 3 blind mice! I knew that selecting these characters were going to cause a little bit of a stir in the blind community due to it's song lyrics and derogatory depiction of who blind people are. I did my research, I read the origin and I pondered on lyrics to the song 3 blind mice. It is NOT a pleasing song to say the least BUT I decided to change the perception of these mice by reclaiming the characters and making them our own by transforming them into modern hip, happy and positive characters. We meticulously created every character to represent all present and future aspects of Braille Code Inc. My main goal for the 3 Blind Mice is to show that yes they are blind, visually impaired, handsome and cute; they are also smart, confident and willing to persevere through the visual world they live in! They are aware that the things that make them different are same things that makes them special. My brother Pablo and I created names for them and in this book we are introducing: **Kelly Keller** *was inspired in honor of my "shero" Helen Keller.* **Charlie Cane** *was inspired by the cane used for the blind and the confident, sharp-suit-wearing Steve Harvey.* **Bobby Braille** *is a cool, happy musical prodigy that was inspired by Stevie Wonder and Wani. All names were created in relation to the blind world with matching initials.*

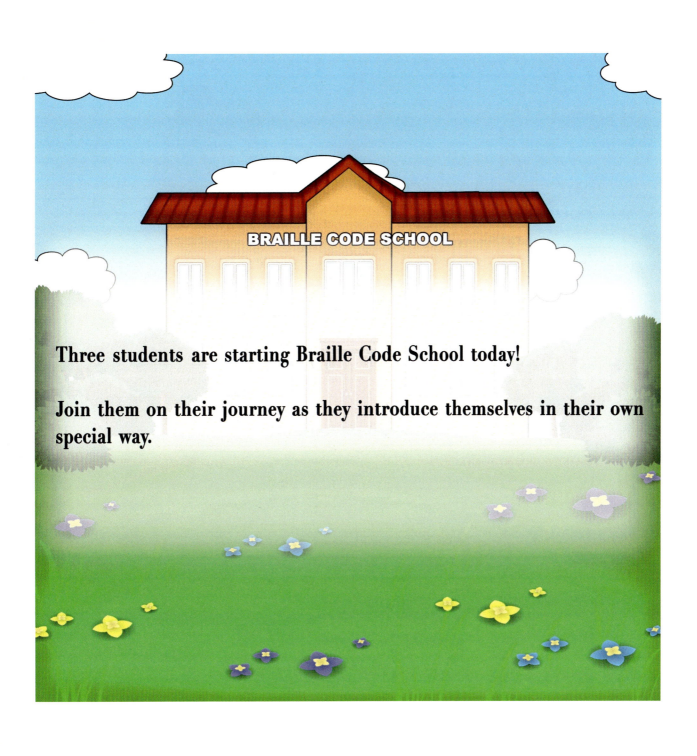

Introducing:

Kelly Keller

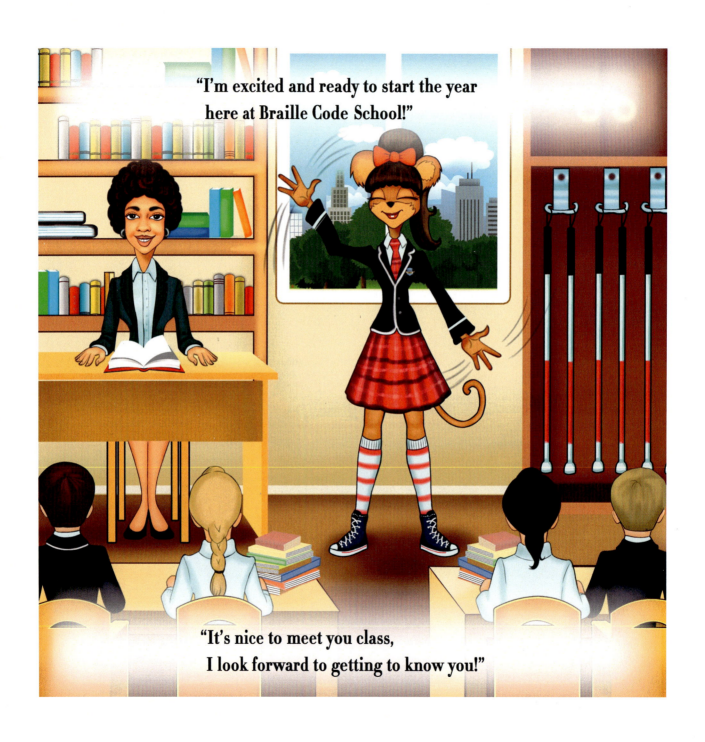

Charlie Cane

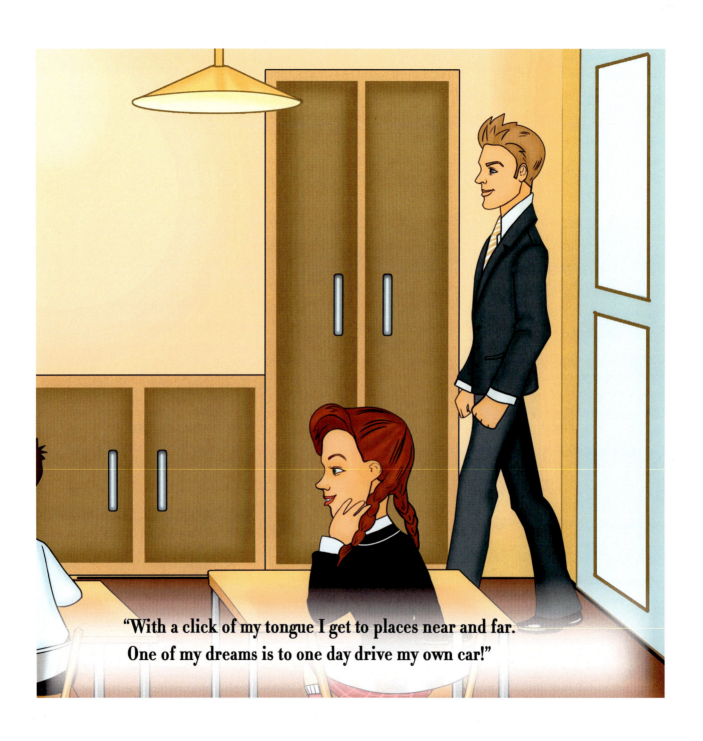

"I want to make history so that people can read about me too.
I want an adventurous life
where many won't believe it's true.

I'm a blind kid, I want to make a difference
and I've only just begun.
I'm ready to meet you all, let's learn,
let's braille, and have some fun!"

"We all have things that we fear but in time we will overcome them all.
We will share our stories be it good or bad and catch each other if we fall.

What is cool about Braille Code School is that at the end of every day,
we do our best "we have what it takes" is what we always say!"

MEET THE AUTHOR

Hello! My name is Gracie and I am the creator and author of "What's Cool About Braille Code School?" My parents are Garifuna, they were born and raised in Honduras, C.A. and I am a first generation born, raised and currently residing in Brooklyn, NY. I'm an entrepreneur, a wife and a mother of three wonderful children! In 2014, the characters: Kelly, Charlie and Bobby were created as a logo for my assistive clothing line for the Blind/Visually Impaired (B/VI) called Braille Code Inc. I did not see any clothes that could help my visually impaired son Wani with getting dressed on his own, so I created patches to put on his clothes to help him. I then decided to write this book because I didn't see many books with characters like him that he could feel encouraged, proud or inspired by. So, on February of 2016 I brought Kelly, Charlie and Bobby to life! I did it to bring joy to parents, teachers, therapists and loved ones who have special children whom they would like to read to or vice versa! This book and the series of books to follow were not written exclusively for B/VI children but for sighted kids as well who are not familiar with what a B/VI child experiences in school or in their daily lives. I've noticed a separation between B/VI and sighted children. Most sighted kids do not know what Braille is! B/VI children are approachable, they are cool and they are just as fun as they are. My mission is to bridge the gap between them through my series of books.

Photo by: Nigel Morris

Glossary

Braille - a system of raised dots that can be read with the fingertips by people who are blind or who have low vision. Teachers, parents, and others who are not visually impaired ordinarily read **braille** with their eyes.

Echolocation - making a sound and determining what objects are nearby based on its echoes. Some blind people use taps or clicks and the resulting sound waves to navigate.

Mount Everest - a mountain on the border of Tibet and Nepal in the central Himalayas. At over 29,000 feet, it is the highest peak in the world.

Inspiring Blind People

Andrea Bocelli - is an accomplished, gifted Italian singer, songwriter and record producer. Born with poor eyesight, Bocelli became completely blind at the age of 12, following a football accident.

Daniel Kish - is an American expert in human echolocation and the President of World Access for the Blind (WAFTB), a California-registered nonprofit organization founded by Kish in 2000. Kish was diagnosed with retinoblastoma, which is an aggressive cancer of the retina, he lost one eye and then the other by the age of 13 months.

Erik Weihenmayer - is an American athlete, adventurer, author, activist, motivational speaker and the first blind person to reach the summit of Mount Everest on May 25, 2001. Weihenmayer was diagnosed with retinoschisis which robbed him of his vision by the age of 13.

BRAILLE ALPHABET

a b c d e f g h i j k l m

n o p q r s t u v w x y z

BRAILLE NUMBERS 1-20

(⠼ is the number sign. The number sign is an indication that a number follows after it)

1 2 3 4 5 6 7 8 9 10

11 12 13 14 15 16 17 18 19 20